Good Morning Lake Jackson

VOLUME II

ELLA ROLLISON SALTER

 www.trafford.com

North America & International
toll-free: 1 888 232 4444 (USA & Canada)
phone: 250 383 6864 • fax: 812 355 4082

CONTENTS

Introduction

Good Morning Lake Jackson Volume II is the continuation of inspirational poetry that is birth through the awakening from my valley experience. The presence of the Lord is voiced through baptism, redemption, mid-night crisis, love and many experiences releasing a message of hope. In moments of despair, disbelief, discouragement, hopelessness, or pessimison, Volume II continuation of inspiration unveils a path that will encourage your inner most spirit. No matter what has come to bring shame or bare blame in your life, "The good news is the bad news is not true!"

The shadow of apparition and the attachment of defeated efforts are now my testimonies that I am an overcomer through Christ Jesus. I now embrace the call of God, to answer and respond willingly in obedience to the move of God in my life.

The awakening to new life in Christ Jesus is my joyful celebration that tells the truth and set the captive free! It is the will of God, that the plan he has for my life is purposed to be uplifting, to minister the penetration of inspiration resurrecting a life changing experience to know without a shadow of doubt, with God all things are possible to them that believe.

Good Morning Lake Jackson Volume II is the birth place of my motto: *I believe in me! I believe in God who believes in me! Therefore, I can do all things through Christ which strengthens me.* Philippians 4:13 (K.J.V.).

Lake Jackson is the physical location of my spiritual burying, *"Therefore we are buried with him by baptism into death: that as Christ was raised up from the dead by the glory of the Father, even so we also should walk in newness of life. For is we have been planted together in the likeness of his death, we shall also be in the likeness of his resurrection"* Romans 6: 4:5 (K.J.V.).

Naturally, Lake Jackson is physically located in Tallahassee, FL along U.S. Highway 27 near Old Bainbridge Road and connects many communities including the entrance of the Meridian Road.

Good Morning Lake Jackson!

6/16/04   5:00 p.m.

Good Morning Lake Jackson!
How well do I remember!
The sight of the awesome sunrise,
It was the fourth Sunday in September!

I'm the eleven year old girl,
That was baptized in Lake Jackson,
The girl, that everybody said would be nobody,
They judge me by my ways and action.

Baptism is not traditional,
It's the confession of my choice,
I was buried beneath your waves,
I do rejoice!

Good Morning Lake Jackson,
And praise God for the awesome sunrise,
It's a mystery to all who knew me,
How you turned my life in you around, into a surprise.

To tell the whole wide world of you,
I am not ashamed,
I've accepted the Lord, as my personal savior,
Its Jesus name I will proclaim.

Being baptized in the Father, the Son, the Holy Ghost,
I'll never forget how to complete I became,
The Landmark on my new life in Christ,
Good Morning Lake Jackson, You washed away the shame.

The Promise
7/9/04   11:00 p.m.

It is an important part
Of all the family relationship,
That one keeps everything in focus
When times in life test the kinship.

My Father made the Promise to me
And it's to all generations,
The Promise, to never leave you,
Nor forsake you, it's for all nations.

When you can't trace the Promise
The character is in your make up,
Faith, Love, Trust, Patience and Joy
The real connection causes you to mount up.

Be still and know who you are
Wait in the Spirit, you are being lead,
The Promise has sealed you,
You are protected, He's handling it instead.

Every need is being met
You will not experience any lack,
The Promise will always be fulfilled,
Don't panic, don't think of looking back.

The Promise, The love, my heart
The place of understanding He's never late,
The joy of knowing that in every situation
He works it out, In Obedience I must wait.

The Promise put a smile on my face
His awesome moves are excellent,
It blessed me beyond measure
He shows up, and I say present.

The Promise has never been broken
He is the Word; The Word is always the same.
The Word Promise, Promise the Word,
With power and authority in Jesus Name.

The White House Should Be Called The Black House!

7/10/04   1:30 a.m.

The capitol of the United States of America
The location of the White House,
The Place where the laws are made and broken,
The office where the president acts like a mouse.

The White House has so much security
To keep the crooks, criminal and terrorist out.
The silent place for hidden secrets
The noises place when the mouse moves about.

The White House should be called the Black House
For all the dirt that they dig,
They fight like cats and dogs for positions
It doesn't matter if you are bald or wear a wig.

As long as you can stay in the race
The longer the competition will search your pass,
They don't care what dirt show up
All they want is a chance to kick your ass.

The White House should be called the Black House
For the thief, the murder and the schemer,
Sits in the Oval Office with a deviant heart,
Plotting and planning while others are dreamers.

The successor never forget the errors
The ones you called a mistake,
The White House should be called the Black House
At any given time, you'll get set up, because of a date
you make.

The White House can't hold the light
To trouble the minority invents,
They walk over pennies and had no records,
On how millions, Trillions of dollars are spent.

To the Ghetto Communities statewide
The foundation has been set,
The greatest role models are the leaders
The ones that won the election, that's what we get.

The White should be called the Black House
For all the hidden secrets and covered up lies,
Some are established while America sleeps,
To try to outsmart the spies.

The Friday Blues!

7/12/04   2:30 p.m.

I see the happy signs
Talking about life is a beach!
What is it I'm missing?
'Cause I don't smell like a peach.

It seems that you are so happy,
Not every morning, but this one,
When you leave Friday Morning,
I don't see you until your pay check is gone.

You want your home to be happy
Just like you left it on Friday,
But you are missing the point,
This is your home, not a roll in the hay.

You want your money in your pocket,
So you can feel like a big shot,
You want the women to think,
You have it going on, because you got a lot.

The money you make, can't support
The life in the street and home to,
Baby, it's Friday morning again
You got to make a choice on what to do.

If this is how you feel
Baby you got the Friday Night Blues,
On your way home on Monday,
Guess What? I've got the Monday Night Blues.

I cried all week end
Looking for you,
I got a headache
Trying to plan what to do.

The sunshine came out
And dried up all my tears,
Keep your Friday Night Blues
I've been delivered, I have no fears.

The Friday Night Blues will let you down
It will tear your home apart,
When you come to your senses
You'll be left with empty dreams
And a pain in your heart.

Who Would Have Thought!

8/24/04   12:30 p.m.

Who would have thought?
When Martin Luther King had a dream.
That the next century
Would have taken life to the extreme.

When the white children
Would play with the blacks,
That they would still be judged and challenged,
Because they lived across the tracks.

Who would have thought?
A much better way of living,
Would become so stressful
It would lead to violence and killing.

Standing on the Mountain Top
Yes, Martin Luther King viewed the Promised Land,
The way of escape is provided
As long as we obey the Holy Command.

The Dream came to bring hope
The Day of Deliverance, the Year of Jubilee,
To Our Father which art in Heaven
We owe all the praise for the victory.

But, Still, Who would have thought
Our, fine chunky black men,
Would leave their gorgeous wives
To live a homosexual life in sin.

And, Yes, Who would have thought
Our, Sexy, sophisticated children's mom,
Would let their children see so much perverting
That would trouble their minds and cause them harm.

The dream that Martin Luther King had
Was meant to be for our good,
Yet we became so complacency with life
And accepted things we misunderstood.

Who would have thought?
That when dreams come true,
The citizen from the House of Bondage
Would not remember what to do.

The Sinner That Never Spoke

8/3/04   6:00 p.m.

It took a lot for me,
To walk through the church door,
Not knowing who knew me,
Nor remembering me as a whore.

Today is my day of newness,
The step from the old man to the new man,
This day I choose to make a change,
To put my life in the Master's Hand.

As soon as I walked through the door,
Deacon Righteousness dropped his head,
He was, scared to, for I was his whore,
The one he laid with,
When Mother Righteousness pushed him from the bed.

Brother Usher Man heart skipped,
His knees locked, and got cold feet,
He couldn't remember his function as an Usher,
He couldn't show me to my seat.

Mother Always Right had a look,
That would cut me into pieces,
For my appearance disrupted her plan,
Today she couldn't wrinkle the Pastor's creases.

The Choir couldn't sing the song,
That invites the sinner in,
What's the matter with them all?
I'm not living another day in sin.

The Pastor couldn't remember,
The sermon he needed to preach,
As for me, I wasn't concerned about them,
All I wanted was for my soul to be reached.

Isn't it funny, I thought to myself?
How everyone remembered me as whore,
They couldn't get passed it, Afterward,
They soon rushed me out of the door.

We all had something in common,
The familiar spirit called sin,
Why can't we all repent to God?
For right now we are in the same den.

The sinner that never spoke,
It was the past that told the story,
Sadly to know, the mentally of others,
Can't rejoice with you and give God the Glory.

Not Just a Rock!
8/20/04   8:10 a.m.

Such an unusual looking Rock,
Was waiting in a noticeable spot,
It got my attention quickly,
It became mine and I cherish it a lot.

No matter what I am experiencing,
To this Rock my attention is drawn,
Soon after I look and spent time with it,
Not long after my troubles are gone.

Sometimes I feel like who cares,
But wherever I am I look, its there,
To myself I said, not just a Rock!
Whenever I'm to that point,
This Rock is everywhere.

Not just a rock, but the Rock,
My help in every way,
The shelter for me to rest,
When it is a rainy day.

The lifter for my head,
When the weight seems so strong,
The power to my walk,
Guiding me and keeping me from wrong.

Not just a rock, But the Rock,
The Source of all my needs,
The instruction for the harvest,
To reap from my sown seeds.

Such an unusual rock,
Was waiting in a noticeable spot,
Up on the cross at Calvary's Hill,
Saying, "Look to me, what you need I've got!"

A Little Honey! A Little Money!

9/24/04   7:25 p.m.

Two desperate lonely citizens
Always end up talking to each other,
About nothing that means anything
One thing leads to another.

One said to the other,
While standing in the Parking Lot!
I have nothing but time today
We can come to my place and share what we got.

That's a nice idea
They both agreed to share,
Lady you got a little honey
A little money for you is there.

Who would have thought?
Two beautiful citizens well kept,
For a little honey and a little money
Together lonely thy both slept.

Dance Trees Dance
8/16/04 9:30 a.m.

The branches and limbs
On a tree one day-
Begin to enjoy their selves
In a dance called the wind's way.

The wind blew strong,
The branches and limbs waved,
They went back and forth
They danced until the bark was shaved.

The wind blew in a circle
The body of the tree did the twist,
The moves was awesome
The power from the wrist.

Dance Trees Dance!
The wind is playing your song,
You deserve to worship God,
For your needs, He supply all day long.

Wave your branches
And shake your leaves,
You stand in obedience
And your Creator, You please.

So Many Features!
9/04   7:00 a.m.

Sitting on the fence,
A little cat with so many tears,
Caught my attention,
He had worries and fears.

Not knowing what to say,
To a confused creature,
For this little cat
Had so many features.

Why are you crying?
I asked for my understanding,
So many faces, so many questions,
So many are demanding.

What to do and where to go
Everybody is telling me-
I'm a little cat
With four heads don't you see!

Four heads and eight eyes!
Four noses and four sets of lips,
Eight ears and one neck,
That's a lot to see without a nip!

So many faces
So many questions!
So many reasons
To go another directions.

The Parking Lot Ministry!
7/10/04   12:00 p.m.

Often others have question
The action and mannerism of this walk,
Simply the way on display the example of Christ
Is totally the opposite of how one talk?

When you know who lives with in you,
And you believe just what he says,
There is no special place to share about Christ
Where ever I am, He just have his way.

Because I am a City that cannot be hid,
I'm honored to know that my light shines,
It does not take much, but it means much
To declare to others the joy that Jesus is mine.

I've done many things in the Parking Lot,
Along time before my life became new,
My testimony to the world,
Today the powers of the Holy Spirit can change you.

To share about the Joy I've found
It's nothing new today for me,
On my face before my Father
He gives fresh bread, to keep walking in Liberty.

I love the Parking Lot Ministry,
There are no secrets withheld,
The truth is carefully unlocked
And freedom in the Spirit prevails.

Where can I go to lift Jesus Up?
From this earth, so the world may see,
The Parking Lot Ministry is the place,
Where many have accepted Christ and are made free.

The place where burdens are lifted,
Deliverance through the searched out word,
The level that is not too deep
The breakthrough for the understanding of what's heard.

I've heard many things at the Parking Lot Ministry
For there is nothing hidden, that God will not uncover,
There is nothing said in secret, For God will reveal,
The Parking Lot Ministry, The confirmation that God will
deliver.

Redirecting the negative outspoken thoughts,
Bringing into captivity the seed,
Putting the accuser of the brethren to death,
The fire that would burn the dried weed.

It was brought to my attention
In the Spirit on the Lord's Day,
That this is the Parking Lot Ministry,
For certainly this is where God have His way.

Glassy Lips!
7/13/04   5:00 p.m.

On the other side of the room
One can't help but see,
How sparkling your lips are
For they look as sweet as sweet can be.

No one's lip in the room
Looked like yours at all,
I checked every body
I looked from wall to wall.

Some of the smoothest words
Slide perfectly from your mouth,
The attraction of the spirit
The power of the south.

After a quick evaluation
It's a crystal clear view,
You have glassy Lips
No matter whom you talk to.

How sweet the talk
That comes from you,
Seasoned to meet
The answer to what to do.

The Lips display
Such a remembered reflection,
The kind of lips
That will soothe any affection.

Everyone don't have
A special set to get tips,
What is known and is very rare
The Glassy Lips.

Glassy Lips are so powerful
You will almost believe what they say,
The operation that slides out
And you will submit to their way.

Glassy Lips is a hidden game
Only seen with a hidden motive,
Clouds your mind and use you up
Captured the thoughts that you've never noticed.

Glassy Lips get what it wants.
Reflecting an irresistible attachment,
Once you look twice, you are trapped
Over whelmed by unwanted commitment.

Glassy Lips has a spirit
A seducing spirit it carries,
The danger in the glamour
Is hidden if you tarry.

You Thought I Thought My Name Was Stop!
7/14/04   4:30 p.m.

Every time I start to smile
And enjoy the move of God,
I hear the word stop
To me that's very odd.

As long as I am waiting
To get the direction,
I hear the word Stop,
When I am lead by instruction.

No matter what I do,
Others have a problem with it,
It displease the atmosphere
I'm not a person who only wants to sit.

After having to start over
Again and again I start,
The side standing watchers
Say the word stop, it comes from the heart.

You thought I thought my name was stop!
Someone is confused about destiny,
There is a plan for my life,
I have been predestinated whom I'll be.

Hi There Shadow!

7/25/04   12:00 a.m.

Hi There, You!
You follow me into the moonlight,
You tip toe so softly,
To make sure everything is alright.

You don't miss a move
My turns, my stops and goes,
It don't matter at all
Whenever, whatever, you know.

Hi There, Shadow!
You are in my moonlight!
The expression of the Glory of God!
My shadow is never out of sight.

Shadow with me, near not far,
Your company walks beside me,
Once again I look at you,
From the moonlight my shadow I see!

Hi There, My shadow!
You're there each step of the way,
When the moonlight speaks to me,
My shadow you're there while I pray.

You Had Me In Mind!

8/2/04   7:00 p.m.

Lord you had me in mind,
When you made the birds to sing,
You knew, there would be places to go,
Your songs would have joy to bring.

Lord you cause the lily to bloom,
In the meadows, all through the valley,
You had me in mind to encourage the one,
For those who has fallen in the alley.

Just like the calm stream
So soothing to the thirsty deer,
You have a purpose in mind,
Have faith I'm not far I am near.

You had me in mind,
For you know the plan for me,
It's impossible for me to live without you,
Only you hold the success of my destiny.

The storms, the drought and the famines too,
The opportunity for your greatness,
You had me on your mind in praise,
For you knew I'd magnify you in all business.

When The Tree Shake!
8/2/04   7:30 p.m.

No matter how tall the tree get,
Nor how long the branches grow,
Not like the mind of man
Honor, Glory and Praise to the creator it knows.

So often it is important
To come together as one,
To be sheltered in life
To be kept on the race we run.

When time is taken for granted
And all direction points to the sign, dead end,
When the tree shakes
It is than you will know your friend.

When the tree shake,
There is nothing to hold on to,
Everything that has been taken for granted,
Now you can't get what's coming to you.

Don't be disappointed, admit where you are
Repent as boldly as you performed,
That's the only way to stop the tree
From shake during the storm.

Don't Judge Me, You Don't Know Me!
8/3/04   10:30 p.m.

Every time I do the unexpected
Someone get upset and call a meeting,
Pointing out all the natural reasons,
Why I should be ashamed of my greeting.

Just think, God is moving in my life,
And you can't stand what's going on,
You can't even sleep in bed at night,
For watching to see if I'm home alone.

If I dress up and look real good,
It's a bother to most and to some,
As you judge me, you don't know,
God wants me to prepare for what's to come.

Don't judge me, you don't know
Why I talk to the drunks and the Dips,
The Christian are all blessed and highly favored,
And they are caught up with no time to fellowship.

Breakdowns are essential
If you want to be built up right,
To stand the test of trouble,
To keep you anchored, in the fight.

Smiles are the best friend to others,
Even though the smiles don't understand,
Being judged and labeled to attack,
Don't judge me, you don't know, it's God Command.

Don't Judge Me, you don't know,
You can't begin to master God's will,
All I know is I'm not competing
For many times, I must be still.

So don't judge me, you don't know,
What God is doing for me?
For most times I don't know until it happens
I'm so thankful, through it all, I'm yet free.

A Christian Walk
9/4/04

Sign Language says a lot,
In the presence of a Christian Walk,
It makes a clear statement,
Even if the Christians never talk.

Silence can drive a person
As far as they can go,
Or it may call a person,
To come close and close the door.

The smile can show the heart,
As happy as happy can be!
And the same smile can be deceptive,
A fatal distraction in progress that no one can see.

A Christian Walk in such a way,
The power that's with the feet,
Shod with the Gospel of Peace to change,
The fornicator's mind about who sleep on their sheets.

A Christian Walk should be,
So powerful that it's known,
Not so much about what they wear,
But totally by the seeds that are sown.

My Hip the Meteorologist!
8/7/04   11:00 p.m.

Daily without fail, if I'm not careful,
I almost can tell you when it will rain,
The wind shift me off coarse so quick,
My walk turns into a limp with great pain.

It's not because my shoe is too tight
Nor do they hurt my toe,
It's just the built in alarm
With a certain pinch saying I'm telling you so.

There is not enough pain killers
That can take the pain a way,
It just stays and hangs around long enough,
For you to be thankful and pray.

When the weather has no chance of rain,
It's going to be beautiful and sunny,
There is not a pain in the body
You enjoy shopping and going places to spend money.

When the season begin to change
And winter begin to set in,
My walk has to be pampered and oiled
When I return from where I've been.

Oh yes, My Hip the Meteorologist
It let me know when it's hot or cold,
When it release me how happy I feel,
When it will rain or be cold I am told.

My Hip the Meteorologist
Work just like a clock and on time,
It has never fooled me about the weather,
When it speaks, on it, you can put a dime.

My Long Lost Friend
"Ben Franklin"
8/10/04   2:15 p.m.

I've been asking about you
And no one seem to know which one was you,
But on today, you've made my dream to come true.

I had a desire, a place to be,
No one could help me,
And along came you smiling, saying,
I'll get you there, you'll see.

Ben Franklin,
My Long Lost Friend-
You came through for me,
When the thick got real thin.

All though you'll never around long enough
But someday, I'll have more for me,
So much more than I'll know what to do,
At least for a while, it will keep my mind free.

Thank you for being in my Father's presence
Jehovah Jireh, He is sometimes called,
Just when I needed you the most,
You caught me and never let me fall.

I'm Not Who You Think!
8/12/04

Just because I am obedient
You feel like I am on a string,
Playing the role of a puppet,
Dancing to the beat of your ring.

How sad it is to miss,
The substance of what God gives,
Simply because you are determine
To call the order to how I must live.

I rejoice within my heart,
I'm not who you think,
I'd be less than who I am
If I let you, let me sink.

I'm not who you think,
You may think you can use my brain,
There are always opinions to,
But the final decision my bring you pain

Charley Obeyed God Not Man
8/14/04   11:50 p.m.

All of the wise council men
Came together with an evacuation plan,
They tracked Charley across the gulf,
But Charley obeyed God's command.

350,000 people rushing cross the bridge,
They left the entire bay,
Seeking for a safe shelter
Some where they could stay.

Technology was so accurate,
They knew two hours ahead,
Where Charley would be and go,
But Charley obeyed God instead.

All the wise men
Had to change their plan,
At this point, Charley changed direction,
For Charley obeyed God and not man.

Have not man learned by now.
We can't master God's will,
If we obey Him and seek Him,
We will be kept, if we are still.

Set, Too Bad!

8/20/04   7:30 a.m.

Life is versatile,
At any time the tide may change,
It's up to you to prepare for the move,
However your move, you set the range.

There are so many
Wonderful things to do and see,
Every opportunity you take
Makes exploring a reality.

If pass your nose
Is all you want to smell,
Set, too bad, that's you
I'm achieving, oh well!

I like the clefts
And the rocky edges,
They are new experiences
That requires a sensitive wedge.

It's an awesome feeling
The new things time unfolds,
One must go beyond the horizon
To gain, to have and to hold.

Ella Rollison Salter

When seasons make the changes,
The colors of all shades,
Have you ever pursued the dreams,
How the cool water from a stream is made?

Set in your way,
To do as you please,
Too bad you are stuck,
And don't shift in the breeze.

When you are set, too bad,
Life passes you right on by,
It takes more than faith,
It takes effort to achieve the sky.

Two Inches from the Ground
8/20/04   8:45 a.m.

Two inches from the ground
The voice of a little one speak,
Declaring you are wrong and they are right,
It's not from the voice of the God I seek.

Hoping to establish a new beginning
For the generation of their kind,
Welcome to this brand new time,
You'll change your voice and your mind.

Let me show you the way
The pattern that life expects of you,
For now on as you grow,
And long after you mature.

Two inches from the ground
Such controlling spirit will be destroyed,
Just because of its destruction
You'll save the community, so you can be employed.

You don't understand right now,
Two inches from the ground,
But I promise you, in time to come,
You will be the best in this town.

Two Heads Are Better Than One!

8/20/04   10:45 a.m.

When I was a little girl
The older people would use the phrase,
Two heads are better than one,
I couldn't understand that in my days.

Now that I've lived a little
And learned many things,
What a true proverbs they knew,
For today these proverbs I do cling.

It's not wise to think you know it all,
And in this life you need no one,
Everyone in life have a purpose,
Just be humble and obey God's Son.

Someone else has travel
The road you are on,
You can prevent many mistakes,
Hear and listen as you run.

Two heads are better than one
For one sees the road ahead,
Sometimes we think we got it covered
By your daily word you are lead.

One must pray
As the other head pursue,
Two touching and agreeing,
The Lord in the mist will bring you through.

Two bring balance
A confirmation to God's plan,
The encouragement of endurance,
The Armor Bearer to lift up your head.

The Wind Blew!
10/8/04   11:00 a.m.

The wind blew
So crispy through my hair,
It brought back memories
The thoughts from where.

How times have changed
And life lived now,
Have no sentimental values
Of how love lasted no matter how.

The wind blew
Thoughts from my heart to my head,
Reminding me of the stories,
From the greatest story tellers which are now dead.

Often received with great laughter
But having to make a judgment call,
It's a wonder to know when the wind blow,
It brings life and comforts us all.

You Can't Help!
11/13/04

What make you think I believe you?
And you've never walked in my shoes,
You have studied my culture
And you can't even sing the blues.

You've studied my culture
And an answer you cannot give,
Of how to overcome and conquer,
This tribulation I must live.

Don't tell me how to cook
A pot of peas, rice and neck bone,
When you eat from the drive thru,
And never cook a meal at home.

How do you know it will be alright?
When you don't know what I'm going through,
You are trying to be nice and kind,
Therefore, I pray, that this don't happen to you.

From The Eyes to the Heart!
6/22/04   1:30 p.m.

From the eyes
Of your secret admirer,
Who has satisfied?
Unexplained fulfillment desire.

Often your approval
Melts the heart like butter,
The compliments of taste
Cause the heart to flutter.

It's not what you say
That lets me know you want me,
It's how you say
You are who I'll spend extra time to see.

You seem to know
To make our paths to cross,
And not to long after then
The presence of you in my soul is loss.

No one says to me
Like you do,
How beautiful you are
And I feel it, boo!

The memories of our time
Has the lasting impact,
We best to stop this action
Before we get caught in our track.

From my eyes
To your heart,
What I feel
Can never depart.

A Whisper in My Spirit
12/9/04   11:17 p.m.

I can't imagine what you are going through
Nor how you feel,
One thing I can assure you
That my God is real.

In every situation
We find God appointed will,
He knows it's a shock and understand the pain,
But through it all, He loves you still.

Time, Life and appointments,
We face on our way to destiny,
It's no favoritism nor is it punishment
But this is the way God planned it to be.

To complete the Holy Command
We set love free,
To abide within Paradise,
Forever and eternally.

Love Should Never Be Absent!

12/9/04   11:32 p.m.

Such a beauty, a wonder too,
How in the midst of war, Peace can stand,
To shield the daggers and spears
That is released from the heart of man.

A relationship with the intimacy of God
In the midst of ashes, Arise,
To the amazement of defeat
For the Glory to be revealed in your eyes.

Love should never be absent
It's the wonder to the unbeliever,
It's the destruction for the wicked,
Love is the adversary to the deceiver.

Within my heart abides,
The greatest gift in life,
The Savior born in the world,
Emmanuel, Jesus Christ!

Love should never be absent
The greatest Love story,
That could ever be told,
Unto God belongs all the Glory!

From the presence of life
Set love free through the doors of time,
The pressure to release
All the love that's mine.

May the presence of this love,
Saturate you through and through,
That evens you yourself,
Become amazed at what you do.

Love should never be absent,
Because of whom you are,
For in the Chemistry is a mixture
That has kept you this far.

The Silky Stream!

12/20/04   8:20 a.m.

Walking along the path near a river
Enjoying the peaceful sound of quietness
Brought my attention to a place called
The Silky Stream!

The atmosphere drew me to my knees and soon
I was flat on my face, Captivated in the moment.

A perfect time and place
To release the cares and anxieties, let them go
The sound of the water flow every care away.

The Silky Stream turned all the anxieties into
The mode of a peaceful day.

The Life changing place, The Silky Stream!

Here I Am Again!
12/21/04   12:00 p.m.

Once again, I've been on a trip,
And left you behind with my lip.
Never stop to ask you to be by guide,
Or ask you to show me the way.
How many mistakes I've made
Yet disappointing you every step,
And continued until I hit rock bottom,
Well, Here I am again, Stripped.

Butt naked, no place to go, no one
To turn to, as nice as you've been to
Me each time, by now I should know
I am nothing without you and with
Out you I can do nothing. So here I
Am at your feet, looking up to you
For help. Without your help I can't
See my way neither out nor up. So just this
One more time, Can you help me,
PLEASE?
This time I've learned, to put my
Trust in other things displeases you.
I need you as a friend not an enemy,
For with you I want to honor and agree.
This time I want to get it right,
So, I can stand precious in your sight.

So, Here I am again, Determined to stay on track,
Not listening to my past, not thinking of looking back.
It's now time to take a stand and grow through-
And face each challenge with the strength I have in you.
Here I am with a free mind, with a fresh
start on a new day,
Thankful for another chance, to live in Christ a new way.
Here I am again, reaching up to hold your hand,
Giving you my feet to direct me to the perfect plan.
Keep my eyes so I may see,
What choice I make must be in Thee.
Help my heart not to fail, The test of love,
That I may be comfort by your presence from above.
Here I am again, all of me, I dedicate to you,
This time I've come to know, without you, nothing I can do.

A PRAYER OF REPENTANCE and REDIDCATION!

The Mushroom Season!

1/14/05   10:20 a.m.

If I could write
About the Mushroom Season,
This is a special adventure
To be remembered for many reasons.

Everything for a place,
A place for everything,
No place is complete
Without the joy the Mushroom brings.

The season of the Mushroom,
Journey through and tunnel in,
Capturing every moment
Blending the flavor as it begin.

The Mushroom is not for every dish,
It serves with such sensation,
The preparation that it takes,
Leaves the effectiveness and lasting saturation.

The touch of the Mushroom,
Gently, rest within the warm bowl,
Being creamed from every area within,
Lingering with duration in control.

The Mushroom Season,
Have its pick and its kind,
Never to forget the meals,
For it stays potent within the mind.

The Mushroom has an aroma,
It change the atmosphere,
It calls you in without a thought
To share the moments so dear.

Many places and plenty of times
The Mushroom Seasons rescued me-
From the hanger of death,
To the strength of satisfaction guarantee.

Not a moment too soon,
Nor a minute too late,
The unity for oneness
The solution for the soul mate.

Wise Eyes

9/14/03   3:00 a.m.

In the image of our Father
Just like Him we must be,
Reflecting every movement;
His glorious righteousness for others to see.

In His awesome presence;
Is the school of divine wisdom,
His characteristic measure unfolds,
For the building of His Kingdom.

To the child of God,
You've become the Sons of God,
No one really understand you,
You're not silly, neither are you odd.

Walking in the Spirit,
Is the life path one must take,
Escaping the lust of the flesh
Wise eyes this decision I make.

The crowded road is filled with ideas,
No place for God, Yet plenty to do,
This entrance is open to all each day,
Wise Eyes see, this is a trap to fool you.

Oh Dam!

1/6/04   12:42 a.m.

You hold back the challenge
That I'm not prepared to meet,
Unmeasured pressures redirected,
That would wash me off my feet.

Oh Dam, How smart you are
How strong and caring,
For nothing within your boundary
Is a threat or is daring.

Oh dam, you are the Promise
To hold back the things I don't believe,
No matter how I try to react
It's not mine, you want let me receive.

Oh Dam! It is a pleasure
To have you in my life,
So well protected from the whelms
That I may remain a Virtuous Wife.

You Make Me Scared
9/11/04   9:00 p.m.

You make me scared
When I look at you,
And I see that your
Eyes are closed.

I don't know what
You are thinking,
And it makes me scared
And I can't take a dose.

You make me scared
With your eyes closed,
And you want say a word,
Nor make a sound,

How am to know
What you want, how you feel,
Or what you need,
To be loosed from this bound.

All I know at this point,
If you make me scared,
I'm uncomfortable with
This cold, cold atmosphere,

You make me scared
Just me and you,
You make me scared,
We're the only ones here.

Just Because You Are Mom

12/2/04   6:30 a.m.

It does not matter
How far we may live apart!
There is a special place
A place of love that lives in my heart

You didn't put the love there
For it is an anointed gift,
The Wisdom that you imparts,
Takes me through with a lift,

Just because you are Mom,
You are the most valuable gift to a boy and a girl,
Without you and your Godly instructions
How will I know, How to live in this world?

Thank you for being my Mom
Some may say, Mother, as they call,
You are a blessing not just to your own
But to the lowest, the greatest and the small.

Because you are a gift from God
It is a pleasure to Honor you.
For only a Godly Mother, travails with one
And wait for them to come through.

Just because you are Mom!
So many wonderful treasures in you are found,
The Seed of Faith you minister to the heart,
And soon, there is strength that turns that life around.

Mom, you have a prayerful task,
And abundance of things to accomplish each day,
It's a joy to say, just because you are Mom,
Definitely, you let the Lord guide your way.

Just because you are Mom,
This poem comes to you to say,
It's a blessing to have you in my life,
And I wish you a Blessed and Happy day.

When Daddy Holds the Baby!
12/3/04   5:00 a.m.

The little baby can find
The easiest trouble to get in,
Because he is in his discovery stage,
For his safety, He can't defend.

With tears and anguish
The little one can't explain,
The most unusual thing happened
And now is frighten and in pain.

With its mouth wide open
Screaming with all his might,
Brings Dad to the scene
To take on the mystery and fight.

The helplessness of the child
From the ground daddy embrace,
Surveying the area carefully
To comfort and secure the place.

Daddy picks up the baby
And hold him close to his heart,
Thanking God for his presence
And praying from this child's life,
He'll never depart.

When Daddy holds the baby
His whole outlook on life change,
He is assured without a doubt
His life is safe and is rearranged.

When Momma Takes Her Hat Off!

12/05/04   8:10 p.m.

When Momma takes her hat off
She kneels down to pray,
She pray for the healing of the nation
She prays for the leaders to let God guide the way.

She covers all of the girls
And the little boys to,
She pray for safety and protection
In the things that they do.

She pray for the enemies
Especially for the ones she can't see,
She pray for Salvation
That someday from bondage they would be free.

When Momma takes her hat off
She gets face down to the ground,
She humbles herself and prays
That Satan's kingdom comes down.

She pray for forgiveness
To be in every body's heart,
And that the love of God
Will enter and never depart.

Her prayers are long at times,
Because she loves everybody, everywhere,
When Momma takes her hat off
She is in God's presence, He knows she cares.

Down Through the Years
12/05/04   8:30 p.m.

Down through the years
The Lord has been good,
He has kept me and never left me,
Just like he said He would.

He has watched over me,
And protected my family to,
I just can't praise him enough
For all the things He do.

Danger seen and unseen
Down through the years,
It was only God's love,
Kept me through the tears.

You've been my shelter,
Clothes, water and bread,
My love, strength and hope,
My peace in the storm
And comfort for my head.

Down through the years
My Savior and my guide,
In the midst of the good and the bad,
You've been right by my side.

I wish I could!
"Dedicated to Rebekah M. Salter"
12/07/04   6:00 a.m.

Of all the unkind things,
In life you must face,
I wish I could shield you,
And instantly take your place.

But it would not be fair to you,
For you would never grow,
In God's hand you stand,
And in Him you must come to know.

Of all the unpleasant words,
That people shout out of their hearts,
I wish I could protect you from the purpose,
And the plan that it's to start.

But how would you get experience,
To know wrong from right,
For God has provided us with a choice,
To choose the darkness or the light.

If I could keep you smiling,
And never let you shed a tear,
And if I could hold you tightly,
And protect you from your fears.

But that would not be fair to God
For if I stand between you and Him,
Denying the Glory to be His,
My soul would be destroyed and my life condemn.

Your faith will never be developed,
If I could trust God for you,
What good would it do,
To please God, You need faith.

Beloved, I wish above all things,
That you prosper, be in health,
Even as your soul prospereth (3John 2)
For this is your inheritance for your wealth.

Christmas Is . . .
12/11/04 10:58 p.m.

Christmas is very personal to me,
For I celebrate the birth of Christ,
He's my special gift from God
For He's my Savior, He is my life.

Christmas is very personal to me
The gift that no one else can give,
Wrapped in swaddling clothes
Born to die so I may live.

Christmas is very personal to me
For no gift bought can ever be compared,
To the unconditional love that God gave,
Through Christ Jesus He has prepared.

Christmas is very personal to me
Nothing is more precious than this gift,
For my gift is precious, it's priceless,
My gift is available and is present on every shift.

Christmas is very personal to me,
For I am my Daddy's Child,
For Jesus is my Savior
So merciful, loving meek and mild.

Christmas is very personal to me,
For I live in Christ and He lives in me,
Had it not been for Christmas
I would have no liberty.

Christmas is very personal to me,
It is the birth of God's only begotten Son,
And for every one of my battles,
Through Jesus Christ, they are won.

Jesus Love . . .

If Jesus loves the Children of the world-
Why can't I love all the boys and girls.

They are precious in his sight,
Therefore they must be treated right.

There is a purpose for them today,
So teach them God's way.

Oh yes! Jesus loves me this I know,
Let's enjoy as the little children grow.

Faithful

12/1/03   5:30 a.m.

You are faithful at all time,
What would I do without you?
Every time my back meets the wall,
Some way you take me through.

From the darkest part of my walk,
To the steepest part of the hill,
Before I can give up and faint,
New life comes and strengthens my will.

Oh Yes! My Lord, You are faithful!
Without you where would I be?
You gently walk within my soul
To guide me and keep me safely.

I'm your dear little child,
With my heart open to you,
Your faithfulness gives me trust!
For all times, your word is true.

Seasons

1/6/04   11:30 a.m.

So often I reach for you
Through the encouraging Living Word,
The weight of your world holds you bondage
So nothing said have you heard.

Why be angry at the whole world
For the things you can't control?
Bitter can be better for all,
If you consider the destiny for your soul.

No matter whom you are
Seasons bring about a change,
Don't lose your sense of direction,
Move forward in Jesus name.

This is not the time to be withdrawn
Acting ungodly, with your ups and down,
It takes so less muscles to smile
And far too many muscles to frown.

Seasons has a way with one's heart
To beautify the meek with Salvation,
Don't count God out in your season
What a wonder you'll find in your meditation.

The Secret in the Dew

9/12/03   2:00 p.m.

There is a calmness prepared for me
Early I must rise,
To catch the view and vision
That waits to my surprise.

The voice of my Lord
Speaks so divine and clear,
This is my plans for you today-
Seek me, now! I am not far, I am near.

The secret in the dew,
Settles the confusion of the dust,
Shows you directions to travel,
Blessings will unfold, Follow closely and trust.

The secret in the dew,
Starts with Thanksgiving and Praise,
Which leads into worship?
As I follow in His rays!

Don't panic, don't be alarm
The secret in the dew-
What God does for others
How much more will He do for you?

The Heart without a Song-
9/14/03   1:30 a.m.

Not noticed but unthoughtful
As this may sound-
What a troubled place to be,
In the heart without a song around.

No joy to prime the living water,
That flows with in the belly,
No thank you from the lips of praise,
For this meal of Peanut Butter and Jelly.

The heart without a song,
Is not a cheerful place to be,
Nothing seems to grow very much
Nor respond happily,

The Heart without a song
Has not much hope,
To hold on to your dreams
Or take a jump from the rope.

The Heart without a song,
May seem small with no length,
It has no life, nor breathes to give,
Nor Joy for your strength.

The Heart without a song,
Can be very dark and dim,
For without Christ you can do nothing,
For hope, the light to the world is in him.

Praise ye the Lord,
Everything that have breath,
Lift your head, sing your song,
This is your inheritance to your wealth.

The Breath of Morning!

9/12/03   1:00 p.m.

How appreciative each morning I hear,
The gentle call that wakens me,
Bathe me with such glorious presence,
Arise my child, I have blessed thee.

Renewed strength is upon me,
To carry me through the cares of today!
The breath of Morning is so personal
It's my Divine reward, as I obey!

Replenish nutrients for my soul,
By the still waters I am lead,
Be restored from your head to your feet,
This morning my child, this is your Daily Bread!

I am filled through and through-
With the Breath of Morning,
Thoroughly saturated of the freshness,
Facing each step in Christ, I'm coming!

With much work for me to do,
Today is a brand new place,
Excuse me please, as I enjoy
The Breathe of Morning on my race.

Full Moon
11/04

Full Moon, Full Moon
So high up in the sky!
Will you lead me quietly
As the stars stand by?

The best of the best
Comes out of me,
Rejoicing to the Glory of God,
For all my liberty.

Full Moon, Full Moon
Lead me through the night,
Supply me with Wisdom
To make decisions that is right.

Full Moon, Full Moon
How beautiful you are!
Way up in the sky
Far beyond the star!

Why Be a Crab?
9/5/03 p.m.

From the eyes of a crab
I see that you have so much fun,
Walking in the area, I can't walk,
From the rising to the setting of the sun.

Why is a crab in this beautiful world?
Trading your designer wears for a shell,
To limit your mobility
To get caught and sit in a pail.

In your world
There is so much space,
Yet for me
I'm sold by the case.

Why be a crab
When you have so much freedom?
To receive the invitation
To become heirs to the Kingdom.

Due Seasons

12/28/02   10:00 p.m.

Seasons come and they go
The harvest comes after you sow.

Much work must be done,
Early and late from sun to sun.

Pulling out the look alike weeds,
That was not planted with your seeds.

Plenty of water to strengthen the plants,
To keep them flourish and not look faint.

Due seasons come at God's appointed time,
Be very careful and don't get left behind.

Due seasons bring forth much joy!
When your labor of love in not a toy.

Due seasons has a new beginning,
To change you from losing to winning.

Due seasons are available, but I must wait,
For I shall reap, and not faint.

Winter

12/28/03   10:30 p.m.

Winter comes to take away,
All the infections that can't stay.

Killing it from the very core,
And never to live any more.

Winter had bitter days,
It seems cruel in all of its ways.

The painful moments sometimes we fear,
Everybody is so far away, and no one can hear.

The loneliness has me snow in,
The cave so deep, with no next of kin.

What you want from me and what can I do?
You're not the only one, I'm experiencing winter to.

Winter has a purpose for me,
I'll endue, pray, wait and see.

Winter may not be so bad after all,
I'm being shaped to inherit the fall.

My Very Own Shadow

Every Where I go and
No matter what I do-
It's so funny to me,
That you do the same things to!

You stay with me at all times
We never grow apart,
You are with me when I finish
No matter what I start.

We have the best of laughs
Whether I am right or wrong,
In the midst of living
You stand with me, and I see I'm not alone.

You are my very own shadow,
There's not another like you,
For you are my reflections
Under the beautiful sky so blue!

Great Was The Fall!

5/11/05   11:30 p.m.

It came to my remembrance,
Of the bright sunny day-
When Mr. Jacket, wagon and horse,
Came from the town with bales of hay!

Farming was his passion,
For he had to love it to eat,
No work, No food His Indian wife said,
That's how his life was lived,
To her he was sweet,

As usual he jumps from the wagon to the ground,
To open his raggedy gate,
And walk the dumb horse through,
To put him up before it was late.

Mr. Jacket had a slight interruption,
Taking his unusual path to the stable,
Thank God! His wife became his intercessor,
For His total deliverance, Only God was able.

What really happened was breath taken,
He became missing in action, but not the war,
The saddest thing He had to shut his mouth,
Or become filled with the coated tar.

His wife began to squall and call,
Yelling for help, she called her son!
I was the spy on the bank of the road,
Watching to see what would be done.

Across the field came running,
Uncle Bo Bo to give a hand,
Soon came walking out the cesspool, was Mr. Jacket,
Covered with ka! ka! He took a stand.

Speechless he stood,
Covered with genuine dodo brown-
From that day on everybody knew,
Mr. Jacket as the cesspool clown.

I laugh so hard, I laugh until I cried,
I've never seen a man fall in Ka! Ka!
His wife showered him at the pump,
He stunk so bad, I laugh so hard Ha! Ha!

The best way to describe this scene,
Is to say it was covered well,
Chocolate coated to be exact,
For this story I will forever tell.

Yes, great was the fall,
Ka! Ka! Covered was the outcome!
Thank God it was him—For I was glad,
I was not the one.

I Will Arise

4/15/05   4:00 p.m.

I will arise
And go back home,
I've stayed away,
And I've done wrong.

It cost me much pain,
And my pride,
This road I've traveled,
The path where I have lied.

I am at,
A complete dead end,
In every deed.
I have sin.

I must arise,
I must go back home,
I've been deceived,
And left alone.

From the house of deliverance,
I walked away,
Into a land of bondage,
I went astray.

The invitation
Was exceedingly rewarding,
The consequences was not a thought,
I kept avoiding.

At last I'm awaken,
To come to myself,
Stripped and labeled,
Names by the thief.

I'm still breathing,
So I still have hope to live,
I will arise. Go back home,
Repent, for my Father will forgive.

I Am Not Your Enemy!
2/1.05   10:00 p.m.

The presentation of the truth,
Sometimes comes as a surprise,
It is such a soul revealing matter,
Most times it brings tears to your eyes.

To wound the accuser of the brethren,
Your attack must come unannounced,
The shattering of his holding ground,
Vacated his presence with a bounce.

And now from another office,
The enemy tries to pay back,
To prove He is not at fault,
But that's how the enemy,
Double grip and attack.

To get your undivided attention.
He comes in the form of a deceiver,
A hidden master good at his work,
Talented to make you his believer.

I'm not your enemy,
I come to warn you up front,
Hold your peace, Wait him out,
Soon you'll see him at gun point.

While you are all alone,
At your worried location,
He will reveal himself,
In the secret communication.

You have one thing he wants,
I come to inform you,
Don't sell out to him at all,
'Because nothing he say is true.

He can't love you,
Cause he is filled with hate,
He can't help you,
He doesn't have what it takes.

The enemy wants to tease you,
And make you think he's your friend,
I am not your enemy, I'll tell you,
If you lay and play, you have sinned.

The transition of your life
Can be made brand new,
Confess your sins, and be made free,
For Jesus Christ shed his blood for you.

I am not your enemy,
For I am your friend,
It's in my spirit to love you,
And to say I care, is no sin.

Why Didn't You Leave Me, Before You Got Me?
3/6/05   12:45 a.m.

Why didn't you leave me
Before you got me-
Then there wouldn't be
So much pain and agony.

The piercing force
Within my chest,
Each time I hear
I've made every one's life a mess.

The inconvenience to most,
The bother to be kept by all,
Yet born under weight
What a pity and How small?

I may have needed some milk,
Did you ever think?
A cloth diaper or an outfit,
To be changed when I make a stink.

Tell me this one thing,
Why didn't you leave me-
Before you got me,
You never came back not once to see.

Later you were told,
Your child was born,
It didn't matter to you,
You got your needs met,
And now you are gone.

It never crossed your mind
That I needed to be protected,
During my growing up years,
Nor how bad it may feel,
To experience rejection.

I never knew your voice,
How to respond to corrections,
For the authority I received
Came from another direction.

Why didn't you leave,
Before you got me?
Or did it make your ego rise
To know once again you are debt free.

Free from the baby cry at night
The change of diapers too,
The call for one more bottle to drink,
The sleep of hours so few.

Did it matter how I looked,
On the first day of school,
Was it important to you at all
Who taught me the Golden Rules.

Did you ever think about,
Who would treat me, like you treated me?
How you left me inside my Mom,
Not knowing what I needed so desperately.

How would you feel,
Had some man did me that way,
Would you really care,
Or what would you have to say.

Unfortunately, there is purpose,
And there is a plan for my life,
There is destiny for me and you,
For I've been kept through pain and strife.

It had to be painful,
To live in the state of denial,
For all of the years you missed,
They are kept in the Judgment File.

For if you knew better,
Then better is what you would have done,
I'm not bitter toward you,
I pray you are not rejected, By God's Son.

Rejected Again
3/6/05   7:00 p.m.

It's not easy
To block out the pain,
No can one take back
Words uttered with shame.

Farther and farther it drives,
One to the edge of time,
Praying so sincere
For a peace of heart and mind.

Time has built
Strong wounds and walls,
No matter how negative
The firer calls.

From the corner,
Of my personal security,
With everything, I'll let go,
I want hold on to anxiety.

You may call me anything
Failure to except me for who I am,
Rejection is a way of life,
But I am still humble as a lamb.

Ella Rollison Salter

Rejection for a reason,
And in a special place,
Rejection in life by all, But
To God's only Son I will turn my face.

The time of disappointment
The fate that can't be measured-
How I wonder, what's it like,
To be free to have the hidden treasure.

The Baby Cry!
3/10/05   12:00 a.m.

Hey! Mommy, Where are you?
I'm surrounded by strangers,
These people I've never seen before,
Help me Mommy, I'm in danger1

Where are you? I need you now!
Oh No! You didn't leave me in this incubator,
Mommy they are giving me cold milk,
From a dirty refrigerator.

Mommy, I am so lonely,
Everything now is new for me,
I always thought I'd be with you,
I guess it wasn't meant to be.

Can someone hear my cry?
I'm so cold and very wet!
I've cried so long and now I am weak,
The longer I'm wet, the sicker I get.

I can sleep through the hunger,
But the wet begins to burn,
Please, anybody will do, Hold me,
Just give my body a gentle turn.

The Most Gorgeous Lady I Know!

There you are,
Standing so straight and tall,
With that smile
That captures the look of all.

You are known through the community
As a proud young lady,
No one could out dress you
You were clean and your baby.

She is your image
She is known anywhere,
Whatever you teach her, she learns well
She can duplicate it, even if you're not there.

The most gorgeous lady I know
Teaches her child well,
For that child is very wise,
Home business she will not tell.

She has grown to be gorgeous
A lady of character to impress,
Examples of many, but none like this,
She is the most gorgeous lady I know,
I must confess.

Broken To Be Blessed
8/2/05

For quite some time,
I thought I had it going on,
I thought I had it together,
To my surprise, I was wrong.

My circle of life,
Changed coarse so fast,
It felt like a whirlwind,
Memories of my mistakes from my past.

The more I yield to the Father
Completely I must decrease,
It's the greatest adventure to experience,
For the presence of the Lord to increase.

Broken to be reconstructed
From the death of words,
Of the potent voice spoken
The power of the tongue I've heard.

Broken to be everything
That man thought I could be,
Standing on the Word of God's promise,
I am broken, blessed, and stands in victory.

I Am

3/10/05   12:15 a.m.

I am a new born, an infant left alone,
I never knew my mom on the outside,
Only from the inside where I grew,
Now, I'll never know her in the world so wide.

She dropped me like a dog drops her pups,
I may have other siblings out there,
Within a few days, I'm taken and placed,
With a family, my mom will never no where.

I am an infant born today,
Safe and healthy but homeless,
Is there anyone, out there praying for me,
That my new family would be the best.

Pray that I want ever know,
That I was rejected at my birth,
That my self-esteem will not be scared,
And promote me with values for myself worth.

I am an infant born into this world,
Predestinated by God to bring joy,
And with God's grace and mercy,
I'd be loved dearly whether I'm a girl or boy.

From The Voice of an Infant!
4/28/05   2:00 p.m.

From the voice of an infant,
That whey and did sadly cry-
For a moment it thought
How different life would be,
If I could only fly!

The voice of the infant
Sat so sadly buckled in its seat,
Not noticed hardly, But, It thought,
If I could be included that would be neat.

The marvelous things I could do,
If I could get fifteen minutes of your undivided time,
The things I could show you,
From the discovery of an infant's mind.

A fifteen minute of your touch
From your skin to my skin,
The wonderful deposit of life,
That would change my life from within.

Just your eyes alone,
Focus to my eyes, I could follow you,
I could learn things in life,
Quickly I'd catch on and learn what to do.

If I could get that powder formula seasoned
With a little infant oatmeal or rice,
How that would make me stronger,
Then my attitude would be twice as nice.

All I'm missing in life is love,
The voice of an infant abandon and rejected,
Discovered by the Stone Rolling Family,
I became the dollar bill and am not investigated.

The voice of an infant,
Has great potential if given a chance,
Some one! Any One! Make an assessment please!
Let me show you I can do more than a song and a dance.

Those negative words hurt me!
What? You think I can't hear and feel?
My self-esteem would really excel,
So stop! I plead the blood, my self-esteem you will not steal.

From the voice of an infant,
I have a gift to, and I am blessed,
So while you are passing me by-
One day, I will give you a lift from your mess!

Always Remember

5/23/05   1:00 a.m.

When my voice is hushed,
And cannot be heard,
Always remember,
This important word.

No matter where you are,
In this life, Jesus care-
No place you can run to,
Or run from, Jesus is there.

Untold secrets are not hid,
For it wrinkles the heart,
You are never alone, for it is Jesus
Who knows your inward part.

The negative things that happens in life,
Can be for the good or for the bad,
Be encouraged, it's a test so you'll know,
Jesus is your friend, He'll make you glad.

Though you may experience
The pain of rejection and to the curve you are shoved
Always remember this important word,
In Christ Jesus, You are loved.

When my voice is hushed,
Remember this gentle thought,
You are redeemed by the hand of the Lord,
With his blood you are bought.

You are never alone,
The Lord thy God is with you-
When my voice is hushed, remember
Jesus is the way and is true.

You are cared for,
All your needs are met,
Provision for you is made,
Trust the Lord, You will not regret.

Always remember these words,
No matter what others do or say,
I promise you—Jesus Loves You!
It is love that turns the dark into day.

Don't forget, In Christ Jesus
You are a Holy Nation,
You must declare your testimony
From generation to generation.

When my voice is hushed,
Always remember,
That Jesus Blood, never loose its power,
It's good from January through December.

The Presence of You!
1/31/05   7:15 a.m.

It does not take long
To sense the presence of you,
For in your presence
Your fragrance makes me new.

The inspiration is so captivating
With joy beyond measures,
Your spirit mounts me up,
Into the wonders of your treasures.

The transformation is indescribable
In the midst where others are,
You fragrance me with your presence,
You are more than a personal star.

No other spirit can release the favor
The mystery to know you in a personal way,
How I worship and adore you,
For ever I want to with you stay.

You take away my heaviness
The presence of you,
Makes me carefree, you dance with me,
Until I come through.

The presence of you
Cannot be describe in detail words,
It is personal, your presence
Your love for me no other voice I've heard.

The Only Man My Mother Ever Loved!
2/21/05   9:30 p.m.

The only man my mother ever loved,
Put a look on her face,
That made her heart happy,
She sang all day long, His Amazing Grace.

When the bread got low,
And the meat was all gone,
She had hope in her Man,
And didn't worry for she was not alone.

She never cried a tear,
Because her Man made her sad,
Words could not express her gratitude,
For the things He did made her glad.

The only man mother loved,
Made her feel like she was the best,
She never worried about a thing,
For He gave her plenty of rest.

I never heard or saw,
Another man knock on her door,
For she always talked about her man,
She let the whole world know.

Every day of the week,
Mother's Man met her needs,
Although as a child I didn't understand,
Reaping from the sown seeds.

My Mother's Man was good to her,
He let her know she was a Queen,
She remain faithful to Him,
And often He raised her self-esteem.

Mother often told us,
About this love in her life,
Her children loved her Man to,
For she was her Man's wife.

The only Man my Mother ever loved,
She loved Him with all of her heart,
She remained faithful to Him,
And from Him She never depart.

He was her Healer, Provider to,
He kept her in each step she took,
He was her Keeper in all things,
There is no other man for Mother,
She refused to look.

The only Man my Mother ever loved,
Did for me, what no other could do,
He became my personal Father,
And is still faithful and is always true.

The only Man my Mother ever loved,
I fell in love with him too,
I believe in Him, Accepted Him, and today,
I introduce my Personal Savior to you!

The Greatest, My Savior,
The rewarded to those who diligently seek Him,
The best friend of all times,
Always, there, through the thick and the thin.

The only man my mother ever loved,
Was the only Man, Her Mother ever loved,
Now, is the only Man I ever loved,
Thank God for sending Jesus from above.

My Light! My Father!
5/8/05   10:55 a.m.

Each step in life requires
Basic Instructions for success,
Not everyone can give them,
For it would complicate life and make a mess.

There are many paths to choose from,
Some may look identical,
When you know your Father's voice
Then it is really authentically.

My direction has such glow,
It shines like no other light,
My Father it belongs to,
And He shows me the path that is right.

Temptation calls out my name,
So loud and strongly I am drawn,
My Light, My Father shields me,
And keep me from the harm.

I don't know which way to go
For I am shown what to do-
The Basic Instruction aluminates,
Those I must follow completely through.

My Light! My Father!
The greatest hero, ever,
Set on His Throne surrounded by Glory,
That's where I'm lead, to be with him, forever.

No other light I've ever known
Can lead you to this place,
And the complexity to the deceiver,
Will then understand the Amazing Grace.

My Light! My Father!
Where you pass will never be traced,
For the presence of the light,
Cause you to endure and complete your race.

You cannot walk in the dark
You cannot see where you are going-
My Light! My Father! Gives the invitation,
To come and follow, For He is all knowing.

My Light! My Father!
My greatest gift of all times,
For everything I need is in him,
My Light! My Father! He is mine.

A Cloud by Day a Pillow of Fire by Night!
5/8/05 11:30 a.m.

Not many look up,
Nor will they look out,
But if you ever get in the wilderness,
You will know what I'm talking about.

Sometimes you need comfort,
You need true inspiration,
There is a cloud by day, Pillow of fire by night,
Filled with great admirations.

Don't forget to look up and look out,
There is a Pillow of Fire by night,
There is a cloud by day,
For everything will be alright.

Many years ago, in a country far away,
Moses heard from God, and led the Israelites,
They didn't understand their travel,
The Cloud by Day, A pillow of Fire by night.

It didn't make any noise,
It showed the only direction,
From bondage to the land of milk and honey,
God lead with divine Instruction.

When the cloud stopped, so did Moses
The Israelites had attitude and began to complain,
They act like Moses wasn't a great leader,
And many things on him they did blame.

The lesson for the future generations,
Was taught through this great leader,
I'd take a divine approach,
To conquer and defeat the deceiver.

God is omnipresence,
The Cloud by day, The Pillow of fire by night,
He is the plan to lead us out of your situation,
He knows your motive weather wrong or right.

In receiving instructions divinely,
There must include some discipline-
Failure to walk by faith and not by sight,
Will leave you with a penalty for your sin.

The Thought of your Presence!

5/18/05   10:00 p.m.

You are so amazing
I fall to my knees,
The sight of your wonders
As you blow through the trees.

The balance in nature,
One seasons at a time,
The thought of your presence,
The blossoms and the blooms of the limes.

It's a divine amazement to man
How only you know all things,
Yet your presence man avoids,
But, it's you that change winter into spring.

The excellence display of your glory,
Bring me to a complete reverence,
For you are greater than any painting,
It's your majesty in your presence.

Your fragrance cannot be traced
Yet you turn the head of all,
We sense your presence in the room,
For you linger from wall to wall.

Men of the Kingdom!
6/05

Father

What It Means To Be A Man Of The Kingdom?

Taught through the written Word,
The example to the World,
The life live with integrity
Proven to every man, woman, boy and girl.

Men of the Kingdom,
The one that seek the Lord's face,
Hearing and knowing God's voice
The one who's mercy endue within our race.

The faith in what God can do
Demonstrating through patience and time,
Maintaining your ways in Christ Jesus!
At all times letting your light shine.

Men of the Kingdom
A Tribute to Father's WHAT IT MEANS TO BE A MAN OF
THE KINGDOM?

K—in: To be a Man of the Kingdom
Is to be in covenant with the King,
Knowing that you are the God of my source!
You are my supplier, you are my everything.

I—mage: To the only Wise God I know,
For a purpose and a reason,
I was made in your image,
O is instant in all season.

N—ews: To be a man of the Kingdom,
O shares the good news!
For God so loved the World,
For the sins of man, Jesus was bruised.

G—lory: Man is the chosen image of God,
Reflecting the authority that gives Glory,
The example to the non-believers,
The testimony to the world of God's redeeming Story.

D—oor: You are the door to my heart,
Through obedience, I receive peace,
I am a right now witness,
You cause the troubled winds to cease.

O-mni-Presence: To recognize that you are Omni Presence
For the earth is yours and everything in it!
Where can I go from you Father?
For you know where I lay and where I sit.

M—ighty: To Thee I lift my hands in praise,
You are mighty in battle, my Refuge in the storm,
To be a man of the Kingdom,
You are my keeper, you shield me from all harm.

Ella Rollison Salter

It is our Father which art in Heaven,
We lift up and adore-
I know you can do anything,
You can tear down and restore!

What does it mean
To be a man of the Kingdom?
Not my will, Oh God! My Father!
But, Thy will be done.

Horne Church Goers!
1/10/05   7:30 a.m.

Sunday after Sunday, The parade continues,
The measure one will take to meet their needs,
The cost it takes to produce the attire of attraction,
Proceeds from the stolen tithe and seeds.

The higher the split,
The lower the cut,
The tighter it fit,
To show more but.

The Horne Church Goers,
Can't get a mate on their own,
They drool from their heart
As they practice and plot at home.

The noticeable timing to exit,
The perfect timing to enter,
Just to catch the prey, eye to eye,
The seating location is the center.

Competition is not a quick battle,
For I want what I want, and that's that,
It doesn't matter what one has to do,
Even if my makeup makes me look like a cat.

Horne Church Goers,
Don't know the danger they stand in,
For temptation drawn a faithful heart,
Into a lustful moment to sin.

Horne Church Goers, Be careful!
The target prey is in God's hand,
The Lord thy God is a Jealous God,
You will be defeated at His command.

Redeemed!
6/6/05   2:49 a.m.

On a dark cloudy day,
A place of no security, filled with danger,
The season for the soul to be harvested,
To be redeemed from the clutch of the stranger.

The battle was own,
The victory had been given,
The redemption of my soul,
Has now been forgiven.

Only God know the plan for me
Although the stranger had a plot,
To be redeemed in time,
Blew the enemies thoughts of who's who he forgot.

Redeemed from the hands of the enemy,
Redeemed to give God all the Glory,
The showcase of the power of God,
The banner of victory from the tragic story.

Redeemed in time to testify,
That the test is in the promotion as we grow,
The overcoming of distractions,
Can only be humbled, by the one who knows.

The Pea Liquor!
4/21/05

The older head always knew,
What is best for a child,
Especially those with unusual birth weight,
Born to be losing and buck wild!

I was a little baby,
Born at three or four pounds,
Too small to be left alone
Not big enough to take to town.

From the days gone by
Families knew how to survive,
It didn't matter how small the baby,
The family recipe kept the baby alive.

The Pea Liquor I grew up on,
Didn't make you drunk at all,
It was good for all the babies,
Whether they was great or small.

This Pea Liquor came through the generations,
The wisdom of the midwife,
Feed the baby, It will sleep at night,
Don't deprive it of eating, Start early in life.

How can I forget Lake Jackson!
8/27/05   7:00 a.m.

How can I forget Lake Jackson!
The presence of you that Morning,
Riding on the back of the truck,
While the mothers was adorned with singing.

The Prayers of the Righteous were answered
The hour of praise was on-
Satan had been defeated,
For these sinners were forgiven for their wrong.

Rejoicing from the Church
Out to Lake Jackson's River Bank,
All I want to do is cry,
For all my blessings, I want to say Thanks.

Now the Preacher has preached the revival,
The reverence and the fear of God is in the heart,
It took a lot of convincing for me to believe,
With everything I have, I want to hold on to this new start.

As a little child, many years ago-
Before the evil days set in,
I accepted Christ as my Personal Savior,
He forgave me and freed me from my sins.

It's not easy to walk in darkness,
And forget the things my Savior has done,
For his love, I live on daily,
From Him all of my help do come.

How can I ever forget!
That cool, crispy Morning,,
The Fourth Sunday in September
The beauty of you and all the rejoicing.

The banks of Lake Jackson
Was lined with people from everywhere,
It was so amazing, the love, and the joy
Everyone experiencing your presence,
For you were there.

Riding to the river on the back of the truck,
The Mothers was dressed in white,
Singing miles and miles the songs,
The celebration of this new life.

Take me to the water, Take me to the water,
Take me to the water, to be baptized,
What an awesome Hymn, That signifies truth,
A step of faith, the believer does replies.

I love Jesus, I love Jesus,
I Love Jesus, Yes I do,
The confession of my Faith,
Yes, I believe, every word of God is true.

On the morning when I was to be baptized,
The Mothers sang these songs, That Glorified and not
condemned,
Nothing but the Righteous, Nothing but the Righteous,
Nothing but the Righteous, Shall see Him.

The Deacons prayed a Prayer of Thanksgiving,
That brought happy tears from everyone's eyes,
For this is a time of Thanksgiving, for nature
Rejoiced and the heavens had bright blue skies.

How can I forget, that early Morning,
Standing between two Preachers,
Announcing the baptizing, In the Father, The Son
The Holy Ghost, For the Holy Ghost would be my Teacher.

The birds were flying and rejoicing,
They had a praise of their own,
From that day forth for me,
I've never been left alone.

How can I forget, the chilling water,
Fresh and UN disturbed by the fishermen,
For not one fished that morning
Until the completion of God's Plan.

Thinking back over the days
And how the time have changed,
Releasing my voice of Thanksgiving,
For my life, My Savior has re arranged.

Leftover Residue
8/28/05   11:48 p.m.

Just enough leftover residues,
To mess up the plan of the day,
One speck of UN forgiveness
That hinders the blessings on the way.

That's all it take is memories
Of UN forgettable confrontations,
The attachment of lasting wounds
The ones, that causes verbal infections.

The flash back re occurs
Every now and then,
Simply because of the leftover residues,
Resurfaces the where and the when.

Leftover residue is poison in anyone's system,
Everyone should want to forgive,
It reduces the stress of weight
And add longevity so you can live.

Leftover residue from the days of old,
Once was a curse, a total offense
But just the appearance of victim
In you leftover residue stood with defense.

Armed and dangerous a loaded weapon
Anyone with one ounce of leftover residue,
It does not matter who is the bull's eye,
Get in the way, you'll be a target to.

Personal Touch!
11/19/05   9:13 a.m.

There is nothing like a Personal Touch
A touch of inspiration
To be inspired with God's Anointing
The shifting is for your duration.

The Personal Touch change things about you,
Through your tragic and embarrassing times,
Embraces you like a mother would,
To hear his voice and to witness his Super Natural Chimes.

So much pain and hurt
Fills the heart throughout the land,
It's unbelievable sometimes to know,
The Master holds you in his hand.

He speaks tender thoughts into your life
And cause you to mount up and soar,
Released into the wild life of danger,
And wait to rescue you and again He restore.

He gently holds you on the tip of his finger
And show the visions and dreams,
Giving you confidence to achieve
With known impossibilities it seems.

All that you would come to know,
These are journeys of His Command,
To bring Glory and Honor to His name,
A Personal Touch from the Master's Hand.